VICTORIA AND A

*LONDON*
HER MAJESTY'S STATIONERY OFFICE
1952

## NOTE

The pottery illustrated in this booklet is all from a collection which has been gathered together by the Circulation Department of the Museum for use in a travelling exhibition. The bulk of the material has been lent to the Department by the Trustees of the British Museum ; and this has been supplemented by loans from the specialized collections of museums in Taunton, Devizes, Brighton, Dorchester, Oxford (Ashmolean Museum) and Ipswich.

# ENGLISH PREHISTORIC POTTERY

This booklet shows examples of the pottery which was made in this country during a period of about 2,500 years, from the beginning of the Neolithic or New Stone Age to the coming of the Romans. Pottery as we know it played no part in the lives of the wandering hunters and food-collectors who lived during the long preceding ages of the Palaeolithic and Mesolithic periods (the Old and Middle Stone Ages). The knowledge of pottery, or at least its first consistent use, came with the great Neolithic discoveries of agriculture and the domestication of animals, which first enabled men to live in settled communities and laid the basis for all the subsequent arts of civilization. The sequence of British pottery is continued through the later phases of prehistory when human life was enriched by a knowledge of metals, first of bronze and later of iron; until the coming of the Romans brought to this country the sudden impact of a highly organized civilization and with it the beginnings of recorded history.

The pots in this collection have been chosen to represent so far as possible the normal types which are associated with each of the principal phases, and in order to show only 'whole' pots it has been necessary in some cases to build up conjectural restorations from solitary sherds. Most of the examples of Neolithic and Early Iron Age pottery which are illustrated have come from domestic sites. The Bronze Age pottery, on the other hand, has all come from burials, since it is the funerary pottery of this period which is most often encountered and which is best preserved through having been deliberately buried. But whether the pottery has been made for everyday use or for the special purpose of burial, it reflects throughout the purposefulness and unsophisticated vitality of a primitive utilitarian art. The potter's wheel did not come to Britain until the last phase of the Early Iron Age. All the previous pottery was built up by hand—and from the analogy of modern primitive peoples we know that it must nearly always have been by the hands of women.

For the archaeologist the principal significance of the pottery lies in the very fact that it was a product of home or local industry. Pots were not the sort of objects which could be widely traded, and for that reason it is the pottery which provides the surest means of identifying the many groups of peoples who came to this island and their interactions upon each other.

The booklet has been entitled 'English' rather than 'British' Prehistoric Pottery because it was not felt that the scope of the collection could represent the complexities of prehistory in the extreme North and West of Britain. Most of the prehistoric cultures coming from the continent were first established in the South and East of England, whilst those groups which subsequently passed, or were pushed, towards the North and West naturally tended to develop local characteristics. For this reason it is in the lowland zone of England that we have the clearest picture of the sequence of prehistoric cultures, and it is here that we can mostly expect to find the original and 'normal' pottery to form the basis for the study of the prehistoric pottery of Britain as a whole.

H. W.

## Chronology

| | |
|---|---|
| NEOLITHIC PERIOD (or New Stone Age) | About 2500–1900 B.C. |
| EARLY BRONZE AGE | About 1900–1400 B.C. |
| MIDDLE BRONZE AGE | About 1400–1000 B.C. |
| LATE BRONZE AGE | About 1000–450 B.C. |
| EARLY IRON AGE 'A' | From about 450 B.C. |
| EARLY IRON AGE 'B' | From about 250 B.C. |
| EARLY IRON AGE 'C' | From about 75 B.C. |

1. Bowl, with lugs. Ht. 7¼ in. Primary Neolithic (Windmill Hill culture). Conjectural restoration from fragments excavated at Whitehawk Hill near Brighton, Sussex.

2. Bowl, with perforated lugs and incised decoration. Ht. 4¾ in. Primary Neolithic (Windmill Hill culture). Conjectural restoration from fragments excavated at Whitehawk Hill near Brighton. (Sussex Archaeological Collections, vol. lxxi, p. 64, fig. 6.)

3. Bowl, with impressed decoration. Ht. 7 in. Secondary Neolithic (Peterborough culture). Conjectural restoration from a fragment found at Mortlake, Surrey.

*Lent by the Trustees of the British Museum (Restoration by the Victoria and Albert Museum)*     B.M.63

4. Grooved-ware bowl, with impressed and grooved decoration. Ht. 4⅛ in. Secondary Neolithic (Rinyo-Clacton culture). Conjectural restoration from fragments found at Creeting St. Mary, Suffolk.

*Lent by the Ipswich Corporation Museum (Restoration by the Victoria and Albert Museum)*     *Ip.M.1*

5. Beaker type 'A', with incised and finger-nail decoration. Ht. 9 in. Early Bronze Age. From a barrow on Warter Wold, East Riding, Yorkshire.

6. Beaker type 'B', with cord-impressed decoration. Ht. $5\frac{1}{8}$ in. Early Bronze Age. From the Thames at Mortlake, Surrey.

B.M.66

7. Beaker type 'B/C', with impressed decoration. Ht. 6¾ in. Early Bronze Age. From Goodmanham, East Riding, Yorkshire. (Greenwell, *British Barrows*, xcix, fig. 81.)

8. Food-vessel ('Yorkshire' type), with perforated lugs and with impressed and punctulated decoration. Ht. 4 in. Early Bronze Age. From Goodmanham, East Riding, Yorkshire. (Greenwell, *British Barrows*, cii.)

9. Food-vessel ('Yorkshire' type), with lugs and with impressed and incised decoration. Ht. 5¾ in. Early Bronze Age. From Fowberry, Chatton, Northumberland.

10. Pygmy vessel ('Aldbourne Cup'), with incised and punctulated decoration. Ht. 1⅞ in. Early Bronze Age (Wessex culture).

*Lent by the British Museum B.M.73*

11. Pygmy vessel, with cord-impressed decoration and five perforations. Ht. 1⅝ in. Middle Bronze Age. From a barrow at North Newbold, East Riding, Yorkshire. (*Proc. Soc. Ant.*, 2 Ser. vii, fig. p. 324.)

*Lent by the British Museum B.M.72*

12. Pygmy vessel, with cord-impressed and incised decoration. Ht. 2 in. Middle Bronze Age. From a barrow on Hutton Moor, near Ripon, Yorkshire.

*Lent by the British Museum B.M.71*

13. Overhanging-rim urn, with incised decoration. Ht. 8 in. Middle Bronze Age. From Kempston, Bedfordshire.

14. Overhanging-rim urn, with impressed decoration. Ht. 10½ in. Middle Bronze Age. From a barrow on Bere Regis Down, Dorset.

*Lent by the Trustees of the British Museum (Durden Collection)*      B.M.75

15. Devolved overhanging-rim urn, with cord-impressed decoration. Ht. 13 in. Middle Bronze Age. From a barrow at Sturminster Marshall, Dorset.

16. Collared urn, with cord-impressed decoration. Ht. 14¼ in. Late Bronze Age. From a barrow at Ford, Northumberland. (Greenwell, *British Barrows*, clxxxiv.)

17. Bucket urn, with finger-nail decoration on an applied band. Ht. 14¾ in.
Late Bronze Age (Deverel-Rimbury culture). From a barrow near Winterbourne Stoke, Wiltshire. (*Archaeologia*, vol. xliii, p. 353, pl. xxx, fig. 6.)

18. Globular urn, with perforated lugs and with incised and punctulated decoration. Ht. 9 in. Late Bronze Age (Deverel-Rimbury culture). From a barrow on Winfrith Down, Dorset.

*Lent by the Trustees of the British Museum (Durden Collection)*      *B.M.80*

19. Urn, with impressed decoration. Ht. 5½ in. Late Bronze Age (Deverel-Rimbury culture). From the Rimbury urnfield, Preston, Dorset.

20. Urn, with lugs and finger-nail decoration. Ht. 8⅛ in. Late Bronze Age–
Early Iron Age type. From a barrow near Winterbourne Houghton, Dorset.

*Lent by the Dorset County Museum, Dorchester*                              *Dr.M.1*

21. Jar, with finger-nail decoration. Ht. 5¼ in. Early Iron Age 'A'. From the village site at All Cannings Cross, Wiltshire. (Cunnington, *All Cannings Cross*, pl. 39, fig. 6.)

*Lent by the Wiltshire Archaeological and Natural History Society, Devize*                    D.M.4

22. Jar, with perforated base for straining. Ht. 6 in. Early Iron Age 'A'. From the village site at All Cannings Cross, Wiltshire. (Cunnington, *All Cannings Cross*, pl. 29, fig. 10, pl. 44, fig. 4.)

*Lent by the Wiltshire Archaeological and Natural History Society, Devizes*          D.M.5

23. Bowl, with cordoned decoration, covered in haematite, and with bands of scratched decoration between the cordons. Ht. 3 in. Early Iron Age 'A'. From the village site at All Cannings Cross, Wiltshire. (Cunnington, *All Cannings Cross*, pl. 28, fig. 4, pl. 45, fig. 4.)

*Lent by the Wiltshire Archaeological and Natural History Society, Devizes*          D.M.2

24. Bowl, with grooved decoration and covered with haematite. Ht. 3¾ in. Early Iron Age 'A'. From the village site at All Cannings Cross, Wiltshire. (Cunnington, *All Cannings Cross*, pl. 45, fig. 6.)

*Lent by the Wiltshire Archaeological and Natural History Society, Devizes*          D.M.1

25. Bowl, with incised decoration. Ht. 3½ in. Early Iron Age 'A'. From Dorchester, Oxfordshire.

26. Jar, with bead-rim. Ht. 5½ in. Early Iron Age 'B'. From the Meare lake-village site near Glastonbury, Somerset. (Bulleid and Gray, *Meare Lake Village*, vol. i, p. 32 (P72), pl. xix.)

27. Bowl, with incised decoration. Ht. 3¾ in. Early Iron Age 'B'. From the Meare lake-village site near Glastonbury, Somerset. (Bulleid and Gray, *Meare Lake Village*, vol. i, p. 27 (P29), figs. 5 and 6.)

28. Bowl, with incised decoration. Ht. 4⅞ in. Early Iron Age 'B'. Restoration from fragments excavated at the Meare lake-village site near Glastonbury, Somerset.

*Lent by the Somerset County Museum, Taunton (Restoration by the Victoria and Albert Museum) T.M.6*

29. Pedestal urn, with wheel-turned decoration. Ht. 9¾ in. Early Iron Age 'C'.
From the cremation cemetery at Aylesford, Kent. (*Archaeologia*, vol. lii, p. 329,
pl. vii, fig. 5.)

30. Bowl, with wheel-turned decoration. Ht. 2¾ in. Early Iron Age 'C'. From Bletchley, Buckinghamshire.

31. Bowl, with wheel-turned foot and bead rim. Ht. 3⅞ in. Early Iron Age 'C'. From Jordan Hill, Weymouth, Dorset.

32. Butt-beaker, with wheel-turned and rouletted decoration. Ht. 6¾ in. Early Iron Age 'C'. From Sutton Courtenay, Berkshire.

B.M.86